D1366475

JOURNEY TO THE PAST

# FLORENCE
## IN THE 1400s

Marco Zelasco

and

Pierangelo Zelasco

RAINTREE
STECK-VAUGHN
PUBLISHERS

A Harcourt Company

Austin · New York
www.steck-vaughn.com

Published by Raintree Steck-Vaughn, an imprint of Steck-Vaughn Company

### Library of Congress Cataloging-in-Publication Data

Zelasco, Marco.
   Florence in the 1400s / Marco Zelasco, Pierangelo Zelasco.
     p. cm. — (Journey to the past)
   Includes bibliographical references and index.
   ISBN 0-7398-1957-7
    1. Florence (Italy)—Social life and customs—Juvenile literature. 2. Florence (Italy)—History—1421–1737—Juvenile literature. [1. Florence (Italy)—Social life and customs. 2. Florence (Italy)—History—1421–1737. 3. Italy—Social life and customs. 4. Italy—History—1268–1492.] I. Zelasco, Pierangelo. II. Title. III. Series.

DG735.6 Z45 2001
945'.51—dc21                                        00-045887

*Translated by:* Mary Stuttard
*Editorial Director:* Cristina Cappa Legora
*Editorial Coordinator:* Cristina Drago
*Editor:* Stefano Sibella
*Illustrations:* Aldo Ripamonti
*Cover:* Max Brinkman
*Graphics:* Marco Volpati

*Raintree Steck-Vaughn Staff:* Marion Bracken, Pam Wells
*Project Manager:* Lyda Guz
*Photo Research:* Sarah Fraser

Photo Credits:

P.48 ©Telegraph Colour Library/FPG International; p.49a ©Susan Lapides; p.49b ©C. Stephen Simpson/FPG International; p.50a ©Yamada, Toyohiro/ FPG International; p.50b ©Susan Lapides; p.50c ©VCG/FPG International; pp.51a, 51b ©Susan Lapides.

All other photographs are from the Archives of IGDA.

Printed in Italy

1 2 3 4 5 6 7 8 9   04 03 02 01

# TABLE OF CONTENTS

# All Roads Lead to Florence!

As you approach Florence, you will meet many people going to the very same city as you. Some are merchants, bankers, nobles, and ambassadors from faraway lands. Others are soldiers, artists, and pilgrims. This should not surprise you because the roads to money,

power, trade and commerce, and fashion and culture all pass through Florence.

Florence is one of the most important financial centers in all Europe. Kings borrow money from bankers in Florence to finance their wars. Merchants from all over

the world deal with Florentine merchants as they buy and sell goods from Europe, the East, and Africa. To keep and increase this network of trade, Florentine merchants and bankers have opened branches and agencies in almost all the European countries and the Islamic world—from Paris to Egypt, from London to Seville, from Constantinople to Bruges.

If you are a painter, a sculptor, or a writer, you have come to the right place. Lorenzo the Magnificent lives here. He is an extremely generous patron of art and literature. At his court you will find such important painters as Botticelli, Verrocchio, as well as philospher Marsilio Ficino, and poet Poliziano.

If you really want to be at the height of fashion in Florence, as soon as you arrive go to one of the many excellent tailors who dress the rich and powerful from all over Europe. A silk or woolen suit of clothes made by Florentine craftsmen will be useful if you want to take part in one of numerous social occasions organized by the important Florentine families.

• Prague

Kiev
•

e
na
e

• Ragusa
(Dubrovnik)

e
Naples

Byzantium •
(Constantinople)

o

• Athens

### The Hazards of Travel

*Travel is difficult nowadays. The roads are rough, winding, narrow, and muddy. It takes a long time to reach cities that are not directly connected to each other. In addition, there is always the risk of being attacked and robbed by bandits. When you travel, it is much safer to join a merchant's caravan or an ambassador's group than to travel alone.*

*To reach Florence by sea, land at the port of Pisa, then go up the Arno River on a longboat carrying goods to the city. Do not carry much money with you. Before you set out on your trip, have a banker in your town write out a check that his colleague in Florence will cash for you when you arrive in the city.*

*To judge how long your journey will take, here are some facts. The trip from Paris or Barcelona to Florence by land will take a month. Coming on foot from Avignon or Lyons to Florence will take 20 days. Going from Geneva to Florence will take 15 days.*

# Welcome!

Look! You can already see Florence in the distance! Do not go straight into the city though. The best way to appreciate the sheer beauty of Florence is to enjoy a panoramic view from a hillside. The most beautiful view is from the top of the hill where the Church of the Mount of Olives stands, on the left bank of the Arno River. There you can take in the whole city at a glance.

Immediately you will realize that Florence is completely surrounded by city walls. The walls are the sixth in a series erected since Florence was founded. They are 28,000 feet long and enclose an area of 1,060 acres. The walls run along a 27-feet wide road on the inside and a 54- to 63-feet wide ditch on the outside. A total of 73 watchtowers, each 75-feet high, rise at regular intervals along the 39-feet high walls, which are topped with battlements. The city has 15 gates. You can easily see them because each is more than 100 feet high!

As you look across the Arno River, you

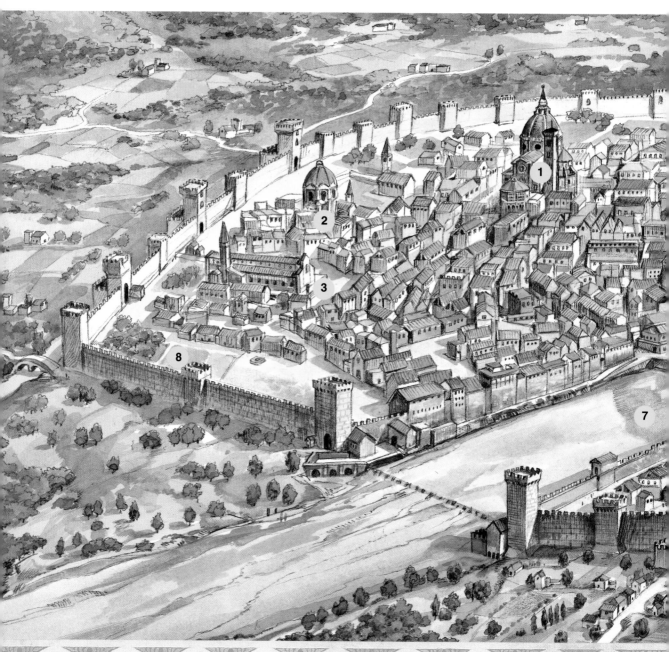

can admire the oldest part of Florence. Your eyes will be drawn first to a huge building, the highest in the city, with an enormous dome and tall bell tower. This is the Cathedral. Now look to its left. You can pick out the Church of San Lorenzo and the Church of Santa Maria Novella. That huge palace topped by a narrow tower is the Palazzo dei Priori, the seat of government. Just behind it, nearer the city walls, is the Church of Santa Croce.

To cross the Arno River, you can use one of the four bridges. The farthest away, as you stand on the hilltop, is the Rubaconte. Next comes the Ponte Vecchio, or the Old Bridge, so distinctive with its small buildings. Then comes Santa Trinita Bridge and finally Carraia Bridge. You may notice that there are plenty of green areas, public gardens, and vegetable gardens.

**1.** Cathedral
**2.** San Lorenzo
**3.** Santa Maria Novella
**4.** Palazzo dei Priori
**5.** Santa Croce
**6.** Ponte Vecchio
**7.** Arno River
**8.** City garden

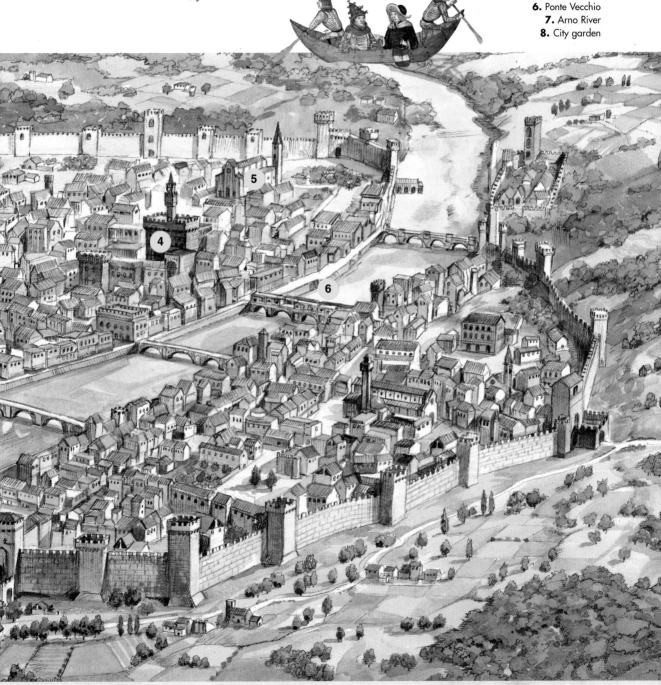

# Useful Information

Once you have come through one of the city gates, walk in the direction of the Cathedral and the Old Market. Most of the streets are straight, crowded with people, and filled with shops—bakers, cobblers, butchers, and blacksmiths. Some of the streets are quite wide while others are narrow, but almost all are flagstone or paved, with an open drain down the middle so that water or other liquids can run off.

As you wander around the city, you will notice that the neighborhoods are not separated into rich and poor. The houses of wealthy people and those of the poor stand side by side. A craftsman's modest house may stand beside a powerful banker's palace.

Head for the busiest parts of the city—the areas in and around the Piazza della Signoria and the Arno River. Florence is not very big; you can walk from one side of the city to the other in half an hour.

The city is divided into four neighborhoods, or quarters. Three are on the right bank of the Arno River. They are San Giovanni, Santa Croce, and Santa Maria Novella. There is only one on the left side of the river. The Florentines are extremely attached to their neighborhoods.

Remember not to carry much money in your pockets while strolling around the city. Coins are heavy and you could easily be robbed. Here is another piece of advice: Do not wander around the city after sunset. There are no street lights and you are likely to meet dangerous criminals.

## FLORENTINE MONEY

The most famous Florentine coin is the gold florin. It is valued all over the world, not just because it always contains the same quantity of gold, but also for the beauty of its design and the precise way that it is minted. On one face is the figure of Saint John the Baptist, the patron saint of Florence. On the reverse is a lily, the symbol of the city of Florence.

The only coins that you will find in local circulation in Florence for buying food and other goods in the shops are denarii, or pennies. They depreciate in value all the time compared with the florin. Right now you need 1,200 denarii for one florin! This is hard on the poor people because prices rise faster than salaries.

You will also hear people talking about soldi and lire. However, these coins have never been minted. They are used just for accounting.

One good thing—the cost of living in Florence is not very high if you just limit yourself to buying local produce such as eggs, greens, fresh fruit, pigeons, wine, oil, and fish from the Arno River.

## WHERE TO FIND FOOD AND LODGING

The best place to stay in Florence is on one of the splendid estates as a guest of a wealthy family. However, it is not difficult to find a moderately priced place to eat and sleep. There are many hotels and inns where you can stay and enjoy some tasty, homemade dishes, such as chopped pork livers or duck in orange juice. The hotels are easy to recognize. They have two signs hanging outside. One shows their name; the other has an eight-pointed star on a silver background, which is the emblem of the hotel managers' guild.

The easiest place to find accommodations for the night is in the Old Market district where there are many excellent inns. Try the Regolina near the Ponte Vecchio, the Osteria del Drago in Maggio Way, or the Bertucce near the Church of San Martino. You will not be disappointed. You might meet artists and writers there. A word of advice: Do not be too fussy. A room may be used by several people, so you may have to share the bed with strangers.

## ADDRESSES AND INTERESTING FACTS

The streets in Florence have names, which makes finding a friend's house or a meeting place relatively easy. But the houses are not numbered, which may give you a few problems. You may have to ask a passerby who may explain with a few gestures that the place you are looking for is after so-and-so's shop, just before you reach the palace belonging to so-and-so. You may lose your way now and again, but with time you will get used to it.

Take care when you are introducing yourself to someone. Remember that Florentines do not use last names. They identify themselves by their first names, followed by their father's first name and that of their grandfather, or their profession, to avoid coincidences and confusion. For example, if you are looking for Lorenzo de' Medici, you have to ask for Lorenzo di Piero di Cosimo, that is, Lorenzo, son of Piero, son of Cosimo. People are often given nicknames according to their jobs. You may hear someone talking about Giovanni il Pecora, or John the Sheep, who is probably a butcher.

## DRESS

If you want to follow the local fashions, this is what you must do. Wear a pair of skintight pants, with legs of two different colors. Put on a short jacket with a belt at the waist that keeps the jacket closed, then add a flowing cape. Complete the outfit with soft calf-high leather boots. You might wear a round, red beret on your head. Another possibility is a *mazzocchio,* a length of woolen cloth twisted and wound around the head in a loose ring, with one end free to fall on a shoulder. At the present time young men wear their hair quite long.

Working-class men wear an old-fashioned jacket that reaches down to the hips and is belted at the waist. They wear a pair of loose, woolen pants. Women wear long, loose silk or woolen dresses, belted at the waist. They add a kind of overgarment in another color. It is shorter than the basic dress and usually sleeveless. They complete the "look" with a wide, hooded cape. Older men wear a *lucco,* or long, elegant gown made of red, black, or purple woolen cloth. It is worn without a belt and has wide, wrist-length sleeves and a hood that is fur-lined in winter.

## WHAT TO DO IN THE CASE OF ILLNESS

The best advice is to take care of yourself! Try not to get sick, absolutely never! The doctors in Florence are members of the *arte* or *corporazione,* that is, a guild or association of doctors and apothecaries. They have studied medicine, arts, and philosophy. They enjoy great political and cultural prestige. You will easily recognize them by their flowing scarlet robes, cap, and gloves, and by the assistant who usually accompanies them. But most are not good doctors!

Florentine doctors use ancient remedies that have been passed down from generation to generation. Their medicines are often extremely bizarre. If you have a stomachache, for example, they may prescribe a powder of crushed pearls. They use salt to help heal very deep wounds. If you are suffering from a high fever, they will plunge you into cold water or they draw your blood.

What about medicine? You can buy medicine in the *spezerie,* or the apothecaries' shops. Apothecaries often ask a doctor to prepare a "miracle cure" from herbs, roots, fruit, or flesh from an animal, such as a dog! Among their herbal remedies they claim that ramerino can cure 22 different ailments. That is wonderful, except that ramerino is nothing more than a common garden plant called rosemary.

Here is another curious fact. Barbers also belong to the doctors' and apothecaries' guild. They are authorized to use their razors not just for shaving beards and cutting hair, but also for making small incisions for bloodletting or for draining abscesses.

Whenever you need a doctor, he will visit you at home, prescribe treatment and medicines, and present you with a very high bill. If you are short of cash, you can go to a hospital where you will be treated.

## WHAT CAN YOU EAT IN FLORENCE ?

Florentines eat two meals a day. *Comestio,* the first meal of the day, is around 11 A.M., and *prandium,* or evening meal, is just before sunset. The common people do not eat much. The basic elements in their diet are bread made from wheat or other cereals, broad beans, string beans, porridge, greens, olive oil, and, of course, wine. Meat and fish are quite expensive and only rich people can afford to eat them regularly. Poor people eat meat and fish only on special holidays or festivals.

Food is prepared for the rich family's table as if for a banquet. There is beef from the Papal States, goats and mutton from the Kingdom of Naples, and fish from the Adriatic Sea. On days of abstinence when the Church expects people not to eat meat, people eat cheese, fruit, greens, and fish.

The State also tries to regulate the eating habits of the Florentines. It may seem strange, but in Florence there are laws that regulate lunch and dinner. One example deals with the number of courses to serve dinner guests. You are not supposed to serve more than two courses of meat or fish. If you break the rule, you are fined 25 florin, which is a heavy fine!

Naturally enough, not everyone follows the laws, and people find ways of getting around them. For example, people make potpies, which appear to be only one dish. Yet they are prepared with several ingredients and can really be nutritious.

So, now you just need to find a good inn, or, if you want to save money, someone willing to invite you to dinner. You might try the famous steak from the Chiana Valley. People say it is delicious.

## WHERE CAN YOU SHOP?

If you have plenty of money, you can buy anything you like in Florence—from local products to articles from faraway lands such as spices, oriental pearls, or splendid Flemish tapestries. You will find whatever you are looking for without much effort. Bakers' ovens, for example, are scattered all over each neighborhood. Why not try Vecchietti's in Ferravecchi Way? At this famous oven, bakers make figures of little men with outstreched arms from bread. Children just love them. As you nibble one, you will realize that it is made without salt, like all types of bread made in Florence.

If you need to go food shopping, go to the Mercato Vecchio, or Old Market, between the Duomo, or Cathedral, and the Palazzo dei Priori. Here you will find a little of everything—from oil to wheat, from meat to fruit, from fish to greens, and from salted meats to chestnuts. At the Mercato Nuovo, or New Market, and along such streets as Calimaluzza and Canto di Vacchereccia that take you to the Arno River and to the Piazza della Signoria, you will find shops and workshops where people sell wool, silk, jewelry, and precious furs—even Siberian squirrel furs.

## WEIGHTS AND MEASURES

You must remember that there are several different systems of measurement in use in Florence. The pound is the unit of weight. It is equal to about 12 ounces. The smallest liquid measure is the *mezzetta,* which is equal to .02 of a fluid ounce. The *barile* is equal to 20 flasks or 11 gallons, when measuring wine. Remember that the unit of measurement for oil is different from the one used for measuring wine: the barrel corresponds to 16 flasks, or 8.8 gallons.

Dry goods such as flour, wheat, and cereals are measured by the quart. A quart is equal to 3/4 of a peck. The bushel is the unit of dry measurement and is worth 3 pecks. The length of cloth is measured in canes, equal to 7.6 feet. What is called "an arm's length of cloth," is equal to one-fourth of a cane. The Florentines calculate distance in miles. One mile is equal to 5,425 feet. Area is measured in the *staioro a corda,* which is equal to 471 square feet, and broken into arms' lengths of 3.3 square feet.

## MEASURING TIME: HOURS AND CALENDARS

Florentines do not attach great importance to measuring time precisely. Their lives are regulated, however, by the chiming of bells day and night, telling them when to wake up and when to go to sleep, work, or pray. At the end of the day, bells even remind them when it is time to bank the fires in the houses, or cover them with ashes, so that they will burn low during the night to prevent fires.

Florentines still use the calendar invented by Julius Caesar. So their year lasts 365 days and 6 hours. It is divided into 12 months and begins on March 25th, the Feast of the Annunciation, which coincides with the beginning of spring. Working days are interrupted by numerous festivals and public holidays, together with Sundays, Christmas, Easter, the Feast of St. John the Baptist, the patron saint of the city, as well as Carnival and several less important annual celebrations.

Each neighborhood celebrates its own particular patron saint, as do the guilds and brotherhoods. For example, if you want to have your shoes resoled and find all the cobblers closed, it is probably Saint Philip's Day, the patron saint of cobblers!

## CHILDREN IN FLORENCE

As you wander through the city of Florence, you will often hear the joyful cries of children at play. Children love to play at imaginary tournaments using wooden swords or to have water fights. They enjoy playing hide-and-seek or ball, and playing with whistles, tops, toy horses, and dolls.

Starting at the age of five to seven years, Florentine boys go to school, where they learn to read and write. They learn to add by using an abacus, which is a wooden frame with rows of beads that can be slid on wires. The schools are strict and lazy pupils are punished by being beaten.

Craftsmen's sons leave school at a young age to become apprentices in a workshop where they learn a trade. The sons of middle-class families continue their education in schools provided by the city-state of Florence. The sons of the wealthy study at home with a private tutor. By the early age of seven or eight, boys are considered to be little men, ready to enter the active world outside the home. The girls also learn to read and write, but they are taught how to do household chores plus such skills as weaving, embroidery, spinning wool, and sewing. For the children in Florence, childhood does not last very long!

## FLORENTINES, WHAT CURIOUS PEOPLE!

I am sure that you have heard that the Florentines are famous across Europe as artists and poets, merchants and bankers as well as for being people who adore luxury, celebrations, and having a good time. Nevertheless, these same citizens are often inspired by a deep religious spirit to create secular brotherhoods and lay societies in order to improve themselves through prayer and to help needy people. They feed the poor and the beggars, look after the sick, comfort those in prison, bury the dead, and help pilgrims, and members of their brotherhood who may need help.

There are many such brotherhoods in Florence. Each is dedicated to a particular saint and is connected to a church or guild. Their members come from all levels of society. They elect their own governing body, follow precise rules, worship a patron saint, and wear their own colors. A typical example of the charitable spirit present in Florence is the work done by the Society of Saint Mary of the Temple Cross. Another brotherhood is the Neri, or the Blacks, so named because of the color of their cloaks and hoods. They help and comfort those condemned to death from the moment they are sentenced until their execution. They accompany them from the prisons along the Street of the Dissatisfied to the place of execution. On the journey they pray that God pardon both themselves and those condemned to die. Once the execution has been carried out, they bury the body.

# The Duomo

Your long, risky journey is now over and you have reached Florence safe and sound. You might want to visit the Duomo, or Cathedral, to give thanks for arriving safely. You have already seen the Duomo from the hillside. Remember its splendid dome and bell tower that rise and dominate the whole city? The Cathedral's full name is Santa Maria del Fiore, the Cathedral of Florence. It was built between 1296 and 1436. It is really easy to find; anyone will give you directions.

The Cathedral is one of the largest in the world and is built in the form of a Latin cross, that is, a right angled cross with the vertical side longer. The outside is decorated with marble in three colors: green from Prato, white from Carrara, and pink from Maremma. Inside, the Cathedral is divided into three *navata*, or aisles, separated by powerful columns and decorated with the works of famous artists such as Paolo Uccello, Andrea del Castagno, and Lorenzo Ghiberti.

The dome rises above the point where the transept crosses the aisles. It is a masterpiece of engineering and the brainchild of Filippo Brunelleschi. Carrying out the project required enormous courage. No one had ever built a dome 138 feet in diameter. It seemed like an impossible undertaking!

An elegant bell tower, the work of Giotto and other artists, stands beside the Duomo. A narrow spiral staircase of 414 steps leads you to the upper terrace. It is difficult to climb, but well worth the effort because from the top you will be rewarded with a unique view of the city. You will be able to see the whole of Florence together with the green sweep of the surrounding hills.

### Ghiberti's door

*Florentines practice the unusual tradition of having their children baptized in St. John's Baptistry, which stands right in front of the Cathedral, rather than in their own parish church. All three doors of this building are very beautiful, but the one directly opposite the Cathedral is breathtaking!*

*The door has ten splendid square panels made of gilded bronze. The panels are the work of the artist Lorenzo Ghiberti. In each panel this great Florentine goldsmith created a scene from the Old Testament of the Bible. The ten episodes move from the story of Adam and Eve to the story of King Solomon.*

## Splendid and everlasting Cathedrals

In the Middle Ages, the cathedral is the most majestic symbol of a city. It represents the city's power and wealth. That is why the citizens want their cathedral to be magnificent. Its construction is trusted to only the best architects, painters, sculptors, and carpenters. The work is extremely expensive and requires a constant flow of money. If the money runs out, the work is interrupted, even for long periods of time. It often takes centuries to complete such ambitious projects when money is scarce.

# The Palace of Superiors

Piazza della Signoria is the political heart of Florence. A powerful stone building dominates the piazza. Its tower and windows enhance the building and make it look less severe. The elegant tower stands 308-feet tall. Each window in the façade of the building is divided into two equal parts by a thin central column.

The building is known as the Palazzo dei Priori, which means "the Palace of the Superiors." It is the seat of the Signoria, or governing body of the city of Florence. Its eight members, at first called priori, then signori, or "superiors," and the Gonfaloniere, or chief magistrate whom the priori elect, live there. They each live in a palace apartment but take their meals at the same table. They only come out under guards' protection for very serious reasons. These men have many responsibilities.

You may be lucky enough to see the chief magistrate on one of the rare occasions when he leaves the palace, riding majestically on horseback, wearing the *lucco* worn by older men, and with a *mazzocchio* on his head. You will notice that he is escorted by guards carrying huge shields and by servants wearing green uniforms. Elections seem to be held all the time in Florence. For example, the priori only serve for a period of two months, after being chosen by a very complicated system. In the final phases of this process, the names of the citizens who are eligible for the most important positions are placed in a bag and drawn out at random by members of a special commission.

Though Florence is formally a republic, no decision is made without Lorenzo's okay. Furthermore, he controls the electoral system, so the most important public offices are firmly in the hands of his trusted friends.

**THE LOGGIA OF THE SIGNORIA**
The loggia in Piazza dei Priori is the largest in Florence. As you can see on the right of the picture, a loggia is an arched gallery built into or projecting from the side of a building. The one in Piazza dei Priori was designed and built by Andrea Orcagna. Public ceremonies take place here, such as the swearing in of the priori and the chief magistrate. However, at Carnival time or for the May Day festivities, it is not unusual for the Signoria to allow groups of young people to organize dancing competitions in the loggia. They even have panels of judges to decide the winners.

## The Guilds

The arte, or corporazione, is a guild, or trade association. Guilds draw up rules about quality, price, and production techniques. They determine work schedules and salaries for the workers and apprentices in their trade. They appoint self-governing bodies and have a magistrate, a coat of arms, a headquarters, and a patron saint.

There are 21 guilds—seven major guilds and fourteen minor ones. These subdivisions correspond to the difference between the upper and lower middle classes. Many of the poorer craftsmen are excluded from these associations because the membership fee is too high. During the time of Lorenzo the Magnificent, they have lost some of their political power, but they still manage large amounts of money.

# The Procession of Mercy

The most important religious procession of the year is organized to celebrate the day dedicated to St. John the Baptist, the patron saint of Florence. All the clergy take part, including the archbishop. Brotherhoods and lay associations also take part as well as the members of the Signoria and the masters of the guilds. Only a part of the population joins the procession. The Florentines prefer to be spectators in order to see the entire parade.

The procession is not just a religious occasion; it is a whole program of recitations, songs, and above all, performances of religious plays. The event lasts several hours. The procession winds through the streets, which have been decorated for the occasion. From the Cathedral it moves to the Santa Trinita Bridge where it crosses the Arno River. Then it crosses back over the river again on the Ponte Vecchio, or Old Bridge, so that it can return to the Cathedral along a different route.

The best place to view the procession is near the Palazzo del Podesta. It is usually not too crowded there. You will find one of the many groups of participants particularly interesting—the Society of Mercy. The

society has 72 members who all wear long, black robes down to their feet. They conceal their head under a black hood that makes all of them—whether rich or poor—equal.

The Society of Mercy carries its standard with pride. As you can see, the standard is a red cross on a blue background with the initials F.M., for a Latin title that means "Brotherhood of Mercy." The brotherhood certainly deserve the greatest respect. Its members voluntarily help the sick and people in prison. They bury the dead who have no one to do this for them.

### THE PALAZZO DEL PODESTA

The podesta is the chief magistrate, elected annually in Florence. The Palazzo del Podesta is his official seat and the seat of the courts and the prisons. It is a spectacular but severe building, with a narrow tower on one side. It has an impressive inner courtyard, with arcades on three sides. In this building the podesta administers justice. Each time someone is condemned to death a bell rings.

## The Tradition of Names

Over time, the tradition has developed in Florence of giving newborn babies two or three names, chosen exclusively from those traditionally used in the father's family or taken from the list of saints' names. That is why the name Giovanni, or John, is very common. Boys' names are chosen by their fathers. Girls' names are chosen with more freedom and imagination, because their mothers are also allowed to have a say in the choice of name for their daughters.

# The Medici Palace

Now what about visiting the Medici Palace, the splendid house belonging to Lorenzo the Magnificent? It should not be very difficult for you to be invited inside, since you traveled so far. The palace was built for Lorenzo's grandfather, Cosimo, by the architect Michelozzo. Notice its perfect design and the original rough stone wall facing on the first floor. The second floor has smooth stone. On the third floor the wall facing is polished. The effect is achieved by using square-cut pieces of stone to cover the rough bricks.

Notice the elegant *loggia* that is all along one side of the building. Well, what are you waiting for? Go in! It is certainly worth taking a look at the beautiful interior courtyard surrounded by porticos. As you can see, it is decorated with medallions and graphite. This is where Lorenzo spends time with his guests, discussing politics and business. Look up! The windows on the second floor are beautiful, aren't they? Something that really strikes you about this house is the elegant and worldly atmosphere you feel inside.

Marvel at the elegant halls and rooms! They are all richly and tastefully decorated. Many contain important works of art. Look in the chapel. It contains a fresco by Benozzo Gozzoli showing the procession of the Magi, or the Three Wise Men. Look carefully. Notice that some of the figures are actually portraits of members of the Medici family.

### THE MEDICI COMPANY

The financial strength and the perfect organization with which the Medici Company is managed makes it the most important bank in Florence. It has branches in Venice, Pisa, Brussels, Geneva, Lyons, Avignon, London, Milan, and even in Rome, where it acts as the treasury for the Papal States. It is involved in a wide range of commercial and industrial activities. It imports raw materials such as silk and wool that are processed in businesses belonging to the Medici Company itself and then sold in Florence and in the major markets worldwide. The company deals in tapestries, spices, jewels, and other goods.

## The Medici Coat of Arms

The Medici coat of arms is a shield with six bright red balls on a gold background. Three gold fleurs-de-lis, or golden irises, the symbol of the king of France, appear inside one of the balls. What do the balls signify? No one really seems to know for sure. Perhaps the balls are Greek coins. Perhaps they symbolize wounds inflicted on the enemy in battle, as some of Medici family's friends believe. Or, as enemies of the Medici think, they may be medicinal pills.

# The Church of San Lorenzo

Not far from Lorenzo the Magnificent's palace you will find the Church of San Lorenzo, the church of the Medici family. Are you disappointed? Most people are. They expect that at least the facade will be faced in marble, certainly not in such poor-looking brick! But just go inside and you will change your mind immediately. In fact, it is one of the richest and most beautiful churches in the city. Cosimo, Lorenzo's grandfather, entrusted the construction to Filippo Brunelleschi, the architect who built the dome of the Cathedral.

Inside there are three *navate,* or aisles, separated by elegant columns. The columns are surmounted with splendid *capitals.* Light floods into the church from the huge windows in the center nave. Look up at the fabulous ceiling. The total effect is one of serene grandeur. Visit the vestry at the end of the transept. It was decorated by the painter Donatello and holds the Medici family tomb. Isn't it amazing?

By the way, have you noticed that group of men strolling in the aisles? The man in the middle dressed in red is the Prince of Florence himself, Lorenzo de' Medici. Yes, here he is again! As usual he is surrounded by some of the most important men of culture in the city. They are most likely discussing philosophy or literature. Did you know that in addition to being a politician and a banker Lorenzo is also an accomplished poet? The talented Lorenzo wrote the most famous Carnival songs himself.

### The Platonic Academy

*It is not unusual to meet Lorenzo the Magnificent around the city. He is usually in the company of those poets, philosophers, and men of culture who make up the Platonic Academy. Besides Lorenzo himself, some of the other members are important scholars such as doctor Marsilio Ficino, its founder, the aristocrat Giovanni Pico della Mirandola, famous for his astounding memory, and the poets Angelo Poliziano and Luigi Pulci. Through their studies and debates, they are making an enormous impression on the culture of their times. They have no real headquarters for their meetings. Sometimes they meet in Ficino's villa in Careggi, but more often than not, they meet in Lorenzo's palace in Larga Street, or even in an inn.*

# Santa Maria Novella

Why is there such a crowd of people jostling in front of the Church of Santa Maria Novella? Go a little nearer! You will see that they are listening to the preachings of a Dominican friar. You should not be surprised as it is a fairly common occurrence in Florence. The friars can preach where and when they like without having to ask the city authorities for permission. In fact, the authorities encourage the practice. A simple platform is quickly erected, the church bells ring, and the citizens collect in the square.

You will notice that the men are separated from the women by a rope, so take care to stay on the correct side! On one side of the rope men of all ages, rich and poor, soldiers and monks crowd together. On the other side, poor women, middle-class women, and elegant noblewomen stand side by side. Women listen to the sermons most regularly and with great attention. The friar is severely criticizing the attachment to worldy possessions and the outrageous luxury of the wealthy. Look around and you will certainly see that many of those in the audience are members of that same group the monk is condemning so severely. Well, these things can happen in Florence!

Once the sermon is over, visit the splendid church behind you. It is more than a century old, but the facade has only been recently finished by the architect Leon Battista Alberti. He was able to complete the work thanks to a generous donation from the Rucellai family. Ele-

gant columns divide the interior of the church into three aisles. The position of the pillars creates a clever optical illusion that makes the church look much longer than it really is. The builders placed the columns closer together toward the front of the church.

## The hospitals

Poor people who are sick—both from Florence and from outside the city—are treated free of charge in the numerous city hospitals. There is a total of almost 1,000 beds available. Unfortunately the rules of hygiene are quite elementary, the treatment is minimal, and each bed is occupied by at least two sick patients. Santa Maria Nuova is the richest, most important hospital in Florence. All the other hospitals depend on it—San Pagolo Hospital, San Gallo Hospital for Incurable Diseases, and Innocenti, or Foundling, Hospital where abandoned newborn babies are taken in and cared for. Innocenti Hospital is another beautiful building constructed by the architect Brunelleschi.

### The game of *civettino*

*Can people really enjoy hitting each other so very hard? That appears to be true in Florence, where one of the most popular games played by young people involves exactly that. The game is called "civettino." In the game two players take turns standing on each other's feet and hitting each other as hard as possible.*

# A Ball at the Davizzi Palace

Would you like to go to a ball in a fabulous palace belonging to a rich and powerful citizen? Court balls in Florence are not an old tradition. If you ask when they began, the Florentines will explain that Lorenzo the Magnificent introduced the fashion and that the most important families are continuing it.

That may be true because court balls do not seem to exist in other parts of Europe.

You will have to work hard to receive an invitation to one of these celebrations! Try asking a member of the Davizzi family; they have the reputation of being very kind.

Before you enter the palace, have a quick look at the building. Although it looks like a fortress from the outside, it really is a magnificent mansion. This should not surprise you because the style is typical of the 15th century.

Once you reach the reception hall you will meet many young people. Some are dancing; others are sitting and chatting. Their clothes are gorgeous. They are all wearing the latest fashions in a variety of surprising colors—red, blue, green, pale yellow, turquoise, purple, and orange-yellow. Just look at the jewelry that both men and women are wearing!

The hall is lit by numerous candlesticks, and the musicians are sitting on a wooden chest. Now you will have the opportunity to learn the most fashionable dances such as the low dance, the saltarello, the pavane, and the pilgrim's dance. Do not forget to notice the beautiful ceiling and the frescoes on the walls.

## Rich decorations!

*The rooms in the homes of the rich Florentines appear spacious because there is so little furniture—a few chests, several sideboards and cabinets for keeping precious objects, a few tables, high-backed benches and some chairs. Although there is not much furniture, each piece is beautifully made, inlaid, and painted. The four-poster bed is always huge.*

## Courtship

As everyone knows, the best season for courtship is the spring, and the best day is May Day, known in Florence as Calendimaggio, or the festival of beauty and flowers. It is an old Florentine tradition for a young man to begin courting his sweetheart by hanging a garland of flowers on her door. She in turn must then decorate her clothes and hair with the lovely, freshly picked flowers. A wonderful way to conclude this holiday is for the young man to sing a romantic serenade in the moonlight under his girlfriend's window.

# The Marriage Ceremony

Which days are the best for getting married? Florentines believe that the best days are the ones that come just before or just after Saint John's Day. When two young people from rich families marry, the ceremony in which the bride is escorted to the bridegroom's house is interesting and magical. So do not miss it if you have the opportunity to attend. You will know when such a ceremony is about to happen because the actual marriage ceremony will already have been celebrated, as is the custom, in the bride's home, with the wedding ring and an exchange of gifts. Everyone in the city will be talking about it.

The streets through which the procession will pass are decorated with garlands of flowers. Tapestries and drapes will be hung from the windows to mark the celebrations. Find a place as near as possible to where the procession will pass so that you can enjoy a close-up view. Remember that the procession will pass through the streets at sunset. The bridegroom's friends, each elegantly dressed, will go to collect the bride at her home, then accompany her through the city streets, carrying torches. There will be music, songs, and dances. The bride will be dressed in her finest gown and riding a white horse. A young page leads the horse through decorated streets.

**REFINED TABLE MANNERS**
The wealthy Florentines are very refined. This is shown not only by the quality of the foods they eat, but also by their table manners. Some eat using a knife and fork, not with their hands, as is still the case in many other parts of Europe at this time. Wine and water are poured from flasks or jugs directly into goblets made from valuable glass or hard stone with silver stems.

## Wedding Celebrations

The wedding celebrations for rich Florentines are occasions to show off their wealth and luxurious lifestyle. The loggia of the palace or mansion is decorated with flowers, festoons, and carpets. Here the tables are set out for the guests. If there is not enough space for all the guests, a special platform is constructed along the street to enlarge the area of the arcade. A colored awning is erected to protect the guests from the sun during the banquets, which may last for several days. Men and women eat at separate tables. After sunset, the dancing begins. In an area lit by candles and torches, the guests dance late into the night.

# The Old Market

As you walk along Calimala Way, you will be attracted by the continuous buzz of voices. The voices come from the Piazza del Mercato Vecchio, or Old Market Square. This is the commercial center of Florence, the place where the everyday life of the ordinary Florentines is at its most lively and exuberant.

The central building is divided into shops. You will find butchers, bakers, others selling fish, merchants selling cloth and leather goods, and some selling delicatessen products. You will even find cooks preparing delicious meals to sell. Peddlers display their wares such as eggs, pigeons, oil, fruit and vegetables on market stands. Seated on the floor besides their sacks, grain-dealers measure out their goods. Do you need a haircut? In the market you will also find barbers working out in the open air.

But this is not all. The market is the meeting place for all kinds of people, the common people and the middle classes, peasants and merchants, craftsmen and notaries, children and loafers. You will notice that there are many beggars. They use all kinds of devices and tricks to stir up pity from the passersby by showing horrendous deformities that may or may not be real.

There always are jugglers, acrobats, and streetsingers to entertain you. Monks ask for alms for their convent. Cheats and quacks sell mysterious mixtures, which, they claim, have magic powers to provide miraculous cures. Gamblers take great care not to be caught by the guards. You can see the tall Column of Abundance standing in the square and, naturally enough, a well. Water must always be available in a market.

## SHRINES IN FLORENCE

You will find many shrines at street corners, along roads, and at crossroads. A shrine is a small niche in a wall where a painting of the Madonna or one of the saints is placed. Shrines are a typical expression of the religious devotion of the common people. They are meant to commemorate what someone believed was a miracle.

## Public Baths

Only the wealthy have a well to provide them with water inside their palace or mansion. Poor people and minor craftsmen have to collect water in buckets from the public pump. The common people are not terribly hygienic. If you want to take a bath, the inn where you are staying certainly has no bathtub for you. But there is a solution. The city of Florence has a system of public baths. Here you can have a cheap hot bath. They are organized by the local authorities. Men and women go to the public baths on alternate days. So be careful to get the right day!

# The Streets

The daily life of the Florentine people takes place in the narrow, bustling streets around the city center. The ordinary citizens spend most of their day here among the hundreds of shops, peddlers, and women doing the shopping. Watch out! That baker's apprentice carrying the freshly-baked bread might bump into you. What is all that noise? It is the delicatessen owner yelling that his salami is the best in all of Tuscany or the blacksmith beating iron on his anvil! The noise is enough to deafen you!

The two women leaning out from their *sporti*, or covered balcony, exchange the latest gossip as they shout at the tops of their voices. Do not ask that repentant sinner why he is whipping himself with such fervor. He would never answer you because he is so intent on punishing himself for his sins and for all the evil in the world.

People walk up and down, chat, enjoy themselves, and judge the goods on sale with an expert's eye. By all means, stop and buy, but do not forget to haggle over the prices. Florentine shopkeepers are expert salespeople! You will certainly find everything you need. You might even want to buy a snack. A tasty Tuscan sausage can do you no harm!

As you can see, the craftsmen work and sell their goods on the street, with just a small roof overhang for shelter. The shops are very small and the space inside is needed for storing goods and tools. You are right, there is a good deal of noise and confusion, but you must not worry. It is totally normal for the busy streets of Florence.

### The Construction Boom

*As you wander around the city, you will notice the presence of many building sites. After the construction of the Medici Palace, all the wealthy families wanted to build and live in beautiful, prestigious buildings. Building a house is extremely costly. People have to buy land, or buy up groups of houses to demolish. Then they have to trust the work to the best Florentine architects.*

### The Working-Class Houses

The houses belonging to craftsmen and the working classes are different in height, but they are built next to each other, as if they were holding each other up. They form blocks that are separated by narrow lanes called *chiassi* or *chiassetti*. The houses are built from brick and stone and usually have only two stories, although sometimes they have a third or a fourth. The facades are never wider than 1,814 feet, because there is a strange tax on houses in Florence calculated on the number of windows and not the surface area of the building. That is why the houses often go back a long way from the street.

# The Painter's Workshop

Now that you have bought everything you want, why not go into a workshop and look around? There is an interesting one! It is an artist's workshop. He will surely be glad to see you, because friends and interested people often go into the workshops to look at the work in progress and have a chat.

Oh, this is your lucky day! You have entered the workshop of the great painter Botticelli. But do not expect to see a rich man with a paintbrush in his hand. Artists, who belong to the guild of doctors and apothecaries, certainly do not become wealthy from their work. Their fee is calculated according to the size of the work or the number of hours it takes to complete. *Frescoes* are often priced by the foot!

Artists are not always paid in money. Sometimes they are paid all or partially in, for example, sacks of corn, jars of oil, or barrels of wine. Look, the painter is showing his latest effort to a client. The work is not finished yet, but it already looks as if it will be a masterpiece.

Can you see those young men who are grinding colors with pestle? They want to become artists, so they began to work in the master's workshop when they were very young—when they were about seven. They begin as apprentices and then reach the rank of *discepoli,* or disciples. They achieve the title of maestro, or master craftsman, only after many years of hard work. Only then are they allowed to open their own workshop.

## The Mendicant Orders

*In Florence you can meet many monks and nuns—Franciscans, Dominicans, Augustinians, Servites, and Carmelites. It seems that all the Christian religious orders on the Italian peninsula have a church here in Florence. The monasteries and convents, as you have probably noticed during your wanderings through the city, can be found in different neighborhoods.*

### THE APOTHECARY'S SHOPS

Shops known as *spezierie* are the pharmacies of the fourteenth century. They are quite curious places selling a surprising mixture of goods. Herbs and spices used in the preparation of medicines are sold here, but herbs and spices for cooking such as pepper, cinnamon, and cloves are also sold. Spezierie even sell such perfumes as myrrh and incense. All these substances are kept in terra-cotta or wooden pots. Near them in the shop you will find mortars and precision balances. Bunches of flowers hang from the beams in the ceiling. Camomile, mallow, poppies, and herbs often are thought to have miraculous properties. Apothecary shops also sell colors for painters and dyers. But selling poisons is strictly forbidden.

### Transporting wood

*Wood from the forests of Casentino is really valuable. The Arno is used to transport the felled trunks down to the city. The trunks are tied together to form a kind of raft, which the river current carries downstream. However, there is a flaw in the system! Sometimes the trunks work loose and get caught in the middle of the low dams.*

# The Arno River

The Arno River is vitally important to the life of Florence. As you saunter along the riverbanks, you will notice that this is the most densely populated part of the city and also where you find the largest number of craftsmen's workshops. Water is a source of energy and is essential for the manufacture of cloth. This is why the textile workers, especially the dyers, have built their water mills here, together with their *tiratoi,* the places where the cloth is spread out to dry and acquire a desired shape. Water is channeled into the area along the canal that begins before the dam of St. Nicholas and flows back into the Arno beyond a lower bridge.

You may have observed that only small boats carry goods and passengers from one bank of the Arno to the other. River trans-portation is very popular with Florentine merchants because it offers several important advantages compared to sending goods by land. The *navicelli,* or flat-bottomed boats, used for transporting goods along the Arno come up river from the sea loaded with silk, wool, minerals, and spices. However, they must stop at Pugnone at the small port of Prato, all because of the dam.

The same thing happens for the products that come down river from the interior of the country. They are unloaded at the small port near the dam at San Niccolo. Why don't you hire a boat for a trip along the river? Examine the bridges carefully as you pass under them. The Ponte Vecchio is certainly the most beautiful. It is really very distinctive! Have you ever seen such houses built on a bridge?

### Cloth, dyed all the colors of the rainbow!

If you can stand the stench, go inside one of the dyer's workshops on the banks of the Arno. They will be glad to see you because Florentines enjoy bragging to strangers about their skills as craftsmen. You will understand immediately that it is the fabulous colors of the cloth dyed in Florence that make it the most valuable cloth in the European markets. To fix their colors, the craftsmen use a white mineral called *alum*. Lorenzo de' Medici has a monopoly over this production. But just try asking one of the dyers about the techniques they use in their work. They suddenly lose their tongues! The methods used in dying cloth are among the most carefully kept of all the craftsmen's secrets.

# The Carnival

Elephants in Piazza della Signoria, right in front of the Palazzo dei Priori? Yes, of course! It's Carnival time! Elephants take part in the traditional parade of decorated carts and people dressed in costumes. Carnival is one of the most popular events in the Florentine calendar. A large part of the festival is financed by Lorenzo the Magnificent himself, together with the guilds. So, squeeze through the crowds and find yourself a space to watch the show.

Throughout the year all the young people from the same neighborhood meet to plan the parades, celebrations, and the balls. You should know that the Carnival in Florence is so important that even famous artists contribute to its success. They design and make the costumes and masks. They create the wonderful displays on carts, with scenes symbolizing, for example, the triumph of love, or the spring.

The costumes are strikingly splendid, vividly colored and decorated with feathers, theatrical-looking false jewelry, and amusing masks. The rich people dress up too, in very expensive costumes. All is done in the name of ostentation and luxury! At the end of the parade, after sunset, people continue to celebrate with sumptuous feasts, songs and dances, in the light of blazing torches and bonfires.

## THE FESTIVAL OF THE MAGI

On January 6, the spectacular Festival of the Magi, or the Day of the Befana, is celebrated. The festival is organized by the Brotherhood of the Three Kings, so dear to the Medici family. This is something you really should not miss! Each of the Three Kings, or Magi, dressed in oriental costume, sets off on horseback from a different place in the city. They are followed by many uniformed servants, exotic animals and mules, and wagons loaded with precious goods. The three processions meet in the Piazza della Signoria, then move together toward Saint Mark's Convent. There, an elaborate wooden structure decorated with flowers, tapestries, and carpets represents King Herod's Palace.

## The Battle of the Stones

On the day of Berlingaccio, the last Thursday of the Carnival holiday in Florence, gangs of young men grouped around standards, fight with stones to capture a pile of wood that represents the "enemy's" territory. Given the danger of this so called war waged with stones, the authorities have decided to let the concluding battle take place on the Carraia Bridge or the Santa Trinita Bridge. A word of advice: go with the other spectators to watch the final phases of the battle from a safe spot along the banks of the Arno. Then in the evening you can enjoy yourself in the frenzy of songs and dances around the pile of wood that becomes a huge bonfire for the occasion.

# Football

Are you still looking for fun? Good! A football game is about to begin! Perhaps you do not know this game, but it is a very strong tradition in Florence. It happens to be the Medici family's favorite game. The rules are not hard to follow. Ask one of the spectators to explain them to you, so it will be easier to follow the different phases of the game.

Each team has 27 players and they play on a field measuring 172 Florentine arm lengths by 82. The aim is to send the ball over the line at the end of the field either by kicking it or by hitting it with your fist. The players of each team are divided into four groups, each having a different role to play in the game. Fifteen are attacking players,

four are runners who try to obtain the ball to throw it to the attackers, three are defenders, and five are spoilers or destroyers.

Look over there. The two players who are holding an opponent down on the ground are spoilers. It is their job to stop the attackers' progress using any means they can! The fans are wildly enthusiastic in their support. The teams defend the colors of two Florentine neighborhoods and the rivalry is sharp.

The teams also play football in the large squares in front of the Church of Santa Maria Novella and the Church of Santo Spirito. When the match is played in front of Santa Croce, the scene is really lively. At the end of the game, the winners organize a party for the whole neighborhood. Why not join in? You will have a great time!

**JOUSTS AND TOURNAMENTS**

Because the Piazza Santa Croce is so wide, it lends itself to the staging of jousts and tournaments in the best knightly tradition. Spring and winter are the favorite seasons for organizing these events. The young men from the most powerful families wear splendid suits of armor as they face each other in knightly combat on horseback, either one on one, or in teams. The spectators stand behind a wooden fence to watch the competition. Try not to miss this exciting spectacle!

## The Church of Santa Croce

Santa Croce, the church that stands at the end of the square of the same name, was built by the Franciscans. The interior is simple and at the same time majestic. It is 377 feet long and is divided into three aisles. There are two family chapels of exceptional artistic beauty, because they have been completely covered in frescoes by the famous painter Giotto. They belong to the Bardi and Peruzzi families. There is also an inspiring cloister here.

# The Festival and Horse Race

In Florence the Festival of St. John is celebrated on June 24. The whole town is excited. Many people come in from the outlying countryside for the celebration. Every Florentine, regardless of age or social class, began preparations at least two months ago. This is the most important festival of the year for them.

Religious and secular events are organized over a two-day period. In the morning you can attend a church service or take part in one of the many processions of friars or brotherhoods. In the afternoon or evening, there are balls, parades for people dressed in carnival costume, and tournaments, where skilled horsemen challenge each other with swords and lances.

The most exciting moment of the festival takes place on the afternoon of June 25 when the spectacular race of the Berber horses through the narrow streets of the city center takes place. The race attracts a huge crowd of people who may even come from far away. Spectators line the streets along the route of the race.

The horsemen ride bareback and horses often arrive at the finishing line riderless. Unfortunately some riders fall off their horses during the race. The race known as the *palio* is thrilling to watch! When night falls, the city is lit up by bonfires and fireworks.

**THE FESTIVAL AND THE RACE**
Palio dei Berber is the name given to the festival and horse race that honors St. John the Baptist. The word *palio* is used in its ancient meaning. It means "a banner of hand-woven silk bordered with fur that is presented to the winner of a race." Berber reminds people that the race horses were originally Berber horses imported from North Africa. Riders come from all over the Italian peninsula.

## A Festival for Everyone

All Florentines—rich and poor, men and women, young and old, not to mention many people from the surrounding area—enthusiastically participate in the celebrations for the St. John Festival. Nobles in splendid costumes and modest shopkeepers mingle with the crowds in the city, many of whom have come from countries all over Europe. They all unite to celebrate the patron saint of Florence, and in a certain way to honor the city and its inhabitants, too. During these days the festive atmosphere in the city is contagious, so allow yourself to be swept along by the general enthusiasm!

# San Miniato

So you want to go to San Miniato? No problem! The road is well-traveled; everybody knows it. You can even go on foot; you do not need a horse. It is a beautiful walk and not far away. Leave the city by the San Miniato Gate and take the road heading uphill. You will pass through green olive groves and clumps of perfumed irises up to the top of a hill. There you will find the convent church of the Olivetani friars. You will not be the only person traveling along the road. You will certainly meet many peasants working in the fields and several citizens, on foot or on horseback, going to the church to worship.

The basilica stands on the tomb of Saint Miniato, a Christian martyr who was killed by the Romans. The church will appear quite suddenly, protected by its defending wall. It has an attractive facade covered with geometric designs worked in white and green marble. Two special details are a beautiful mosaic and a gilded copper eagle holding a *torsello,* or twisted length of woolen cloth in its talons. This is the coat of arms of the famous *Calimala* Guild, the textile merchants' guild that has administered the church for years.

**THE PRIVATE LOGGIAS**
Many Florentine palaces have a loggia which is like an open sitting room facing the street. The loggia has a roof supported by columns and arches. Here the wealthy citizens like to talk, play, do business, celebrate births, and above all hold celebrations when there is a wedding in the family. You may even see another event take place there. Young men show off their knightly skills on horseback. They charge and break their lances against a target or even against a wall!

There are three aisles inside the church. You can see decorations by several great artists such as Michelozzo, Luca della Robbia, Rossellino, and Pollaiolo. There is a raised altar; beneath the altar is an access to the crypt that contains the bones of the martyr. The marble pulpit and the Byzantine mosaic in the apse are authentic works of art. If you look down at the floor, you will be surprised to recognize the 12 signs of the zodiac as part of its decoration.

## A pastime for the wealthy

If you have the opportunity, take part in one of the favorite pastimes of the wealthy young Florentines—a hunting party. They hunt small deer, hare, and wild boar, on horseback, with dogs. Hunting with falcons is popular, too. Lorenzo the Magnificent has even composed a poem about this.

# Pisa

How exciting! Here you are in Pisa, on a terrace facing the three most beautiful and fascinating monuments in the city. The sight may seem almost unbelievable! You are certainly lucky to be welcomed as the guest of a family that has been recommended by your new Florentine friends! The ride on horseback was not one of the most comfortable and has taken quite a long time, certainly longer than the carrier pigeon used by your hosts in Pisa when they want to send messages over a long distance.

The terrace where you are standing is really the best place to have an overall view of the Duomo, the Baptistry, and the Leaning Tower—all inspired by the same architectural style. It is true that the leaning bell tower is really the original construction, with its cylindrical shape and its six floors of arched galleries.

The tower began to create problems for the architects during its construction. While workers were constructing the third floor, the ground beneath began to settle, or gradually sink. Have you noticed that the top section containing the bells is not in line with the other stories? Do not worry. You can still climb up the tower! It is really worth the effort as it measures 180 feet in height and has a won-

### The typical day of a wealthy Florentine man

The typical wealthy Florentine man rises at daybreak, washes, dresses, and after a short prayer goes to his office, a place where he deals with his business or political duties. In the afternoon he chats with his friends in the garden, if the weather permits. He dines early and then goes to bed.

derful view of the city of Pisa, whose fleet of ships once proudly sailed the Mediterranean Sea, dominating the trade routes.

You will always cherish the memories of Pisa—the Duomo, the fascinating marble decoration of the Baptistry, and, of course, the Leaning Tower.

## The plague feared by everyone

*Every 10 or 15 years of the 13th century, a horrible plague with consequences almost too serious to be imagined broke out. Doctors were powerless against this disease but advised people to take certain precautions to prevent contagion. They suggested bleeding, purges, and closing yourself inside your home to breathe incense.*

### THE FATE OF THE TOWERS

In second century Florence, you could count a total of 150 towers, each up to 240 feet tall. The majority were destroyed in the course of the struggles between different factions in the city. When Florence was declared a republic, people no longer felt the need to build such towers, as they were used chiefly for military purposes. Now only about ten survive, and they are not among the tallest. They are mostly rented out to the local craftsmen who use them as shops, workshops, or storehouses. What an inglorious end!

# The San Frediano Gate

Whether you have decided to travel back to Florence from Pisa on horseback or have chosen to take a longboat back up the river, to re-enter Florence you will have to go along a road made from beaten clay, leading to the mighty San Frediano Gate, in the quarter of Santo Spirito.

A huge crowd is gathering in front of the gate. There are merchants and peasants with carts, and horses and mules loaded with all kinds of goods, all waiting patiently to enter the city. Before they can enter, they have to pay a tax, because here, as at all the other gates to the city, there is a customs post. The man sitting at the table is a *gabellier,* or civil servant, who collects the tax due on goods at a gate of the city. He is protected by an armed guard. He writes down what is brought in and collects the appropriate tax.

A custom tax must be paid on all goods entering the city, from the precious oriental carpets to the Flemish tapestries. The tax is especially high for all basic foodstuffs such as wheat, olive oil, wine, and salt. This results in price increases that the ordinary people do not appreciate. It is important to realize that this system of customs duties works so well that it is the major source of income for the coffers of the city of Florence. There are people who try to cheat the system, but this is difficult to do and the fines are enormous.

## THE CITY GATES OF FLORENCE

Have you ever counted the number of gates there are to enter Florence? There are also the smaller gates and the side entrance gates too. They are used as secret exits in emergencies.
Each gate, which is closed at sunset, has massive wooden winglike doors reinforced with iron sheets and knobs. The doors open onto the main roads leading away from the city. For example, from the San Niccolo Gate you can take the road leading to the Chianti Hills and to Siena. From the Prato Gate you can travel to Pistoia and to the country villa belonging to Lorenzo the Magnificent at Caiano. There is even a gate called the Porta alla Giustizia, or Justice Gate, where those condemned to death are executed. If you go close to one of the gates, you will easily recognize the religious or political symbols used for its decoration.

## The Army and its Weapons

The Florentine army is made up of foreign mercenaries, or hired soldiers, that are lead by courageous and skilled soldiers of fortune. The foreigners may be soldiers from other parts of the Italian peninsula, as well as from other parts of Europe or the rest of the world. Sometimes the soldiers desert to the enemy if they are offered better pay, so it is important to establish a salary that guarantees their loyalty. Soldiers still use the traditional weapons such as lances, swords, and javelins. The French and Gallic bows and the crossbows are highly-respected, since their arrows can pierce even the strongest armor.

# Present-Day Florence

Imagine a city which is one of the most visited in the world, where the old town is small enough to be visited on foot, where the most important monuments can be reached during a 30-minute walk, which contains some of the most fabulous art and architecture in the world, where you can still shop and live on a bridge, eat delicious foods, and where the passion for soccer is still as strong as in the 15th century! This is Florence.

### The Duomo (Cathedral) and the Baptistery (Baptismal Church of St. Giovanni)

The Duomo and the Baptistery stand in the heart of the old city. The Duomo's full name is Santa Maria del Fiore. You will be amazed by its size. It is, in fact, one of the largest churches in the Christian world. It was the symbol of Florence's wealth and power in the 13th and 14th centuries. Gothic in style, it was begun in 1296 and was consecrated in 1436.

Look up at the dome. Imagine being responsible for building such a demanding shape! Designed and built by the architect Brunelleschi, it took 14 years to complete.

Florence is situated almost at the center of the Italian peninsula, 145 miles northwest of Rome. It is surrounded by rolling Tuscan Hills, scattered with villas and farms, vineyards, and orchards. Florence was founded because of its position as a north-south crossing of the Arno River, to and from the three passes through the Appenines, the hills and mountains known as the backbone of Italy.

The city's past remains its present crowning glory. Its buildings are works of art filled with other works of art. Among the most famous of the city's geniuses are Leonardo da Vinci, Michelangelo, Dante, Botticelli, Machiavelli, and Galileo, and its most famous rulers are generations of the Medici family. Lorenzo de' Medici's patronage, or support, of Florentine writers, painters, architects, and craftsmen began the Renaissance.

### The Baptistery

The other building, just to the right of the Duomo, is the Baptistery, the oldest surviving building in Florence. The Baptistery is large because in the 1400's the Florentines held baptisms here only twice a year. The building is famous for its octagonal shape and three, huge, sculptured bronze doors. The most famous, the east door, is a masterpiece of Ghiberti, who took 27 years to complete it.

## Palazzo Vecchio

Here in the Piazza della Signoria, much of Florence's political history was made. The square took its name from the 13th century fortified castle you see here. The Palazzo Vecchio, the Old Palace, was begun in 1299 and was built as the seat of government, which it still is. It is a stern, stone building, five stories high and topped by a balcony with large notches in the walls and holes in the floor. This construction allowed the Florentines to drop boiling oil and other missiles on their enemies! Loggias, like the one to the right of the palace, were mostly used as the family's outdoor living room at weddings, betrothals, and funerals.

## The Medici Palace (Palazzo Medici)

This was the first Renaissance palace, begun by Michelozzo in 1444 on the orders of his friend Cosimo de' Medici, the grandfather of Lorenzo. The Medici family lived here between 1459 and 1540. The exterior is rather massive, but the square, arched courtyard inside, has the Renaissance feel of delicacy and movement. This palace and courtyard was once the seat of Lorenzo the Magnificent's court of philosophers, artists, and poets. You really should not miss a visit to the Medici Family Chapel, on the first floor. Some surprises await you there. You can pick out members of the Medici family in some frescoes, or wall paintings.

### Santa Maria Novella

This photograph shows the 15th century marble facade of the church of Santa Maria Novella. Standing at the end of a square where chariot races once took place, Santa Maria Novella is a vast church, 330 feet long. A clever, new technique was used to make the nave seem longer than it really is. The columns were placed nearer to each other as they approached the altar area. It worked! The church really does appear longer.

### A Street near the Duomo

The streets in the old town of Florence are still narrow, winding alleys, as they were at the time of Lorenzo the Magnificent. The local people still shop there, together with many tourists, so most of the year they are crowded, but more so in the summer months. Street vendors are rare, but there is always noise, bustle, and chatter. The Duomo is visible from many of the streets and the cathedral bells still regulate the lives of the people, although now everyone has clocks and watches!

### The River Arno and the Ponte Vecchio

The Arno River flows through Florence and down to the Mediterranean Sea via Pisa. Two thin streams come down through the town to meet the Arno. One, named the Affrico, rises in the Appenines and is a minor tributary most of the time, but sometimes it rises and ravages the city with terrible results. The last such occasion was in 1966, when many of the wonderful historical buildings were seriously damaged, and some of their priceless art treasures were ruined or lost forever.

Here you see several of the bridges crossing the Arno in Flo-

rence. The nearest bridge is the famous Ponte Vecchio, The Old Bridge, as it is today. It is one of the most famous bridges in the world. As its name suggests, it is the oldest bridge in Florence. Throughout history it has been rebuilt several times. Its curious silhouette is created by the goldsmiths', silversmiths', and jewelers' shops there. The bridge has a picturesque, hodge-podge air. It is certainly one of the most entertaining, if not one of the most visited parts of this lovely city.

## The Church of Santa Croce

The famous church and cloisters of Santa Croce, which means the "Sainted Cross," faces one of the oldest squares in the city of Florence. Dating from the Middle Ages, it was considered the ideal place for meetings and preaching. In the Renaissance it was the site of tournaments and later football matches.

This type of football is still played here. Santa Croce measures 140 feet by 130 feet and was built mainly for preaching sermons to a huge congregation. The church was constructed in the 14th century. Its walls are lined with tombs of and monuments to world-famous Florentines, including Michelangelo and Galileo, who are buried here.

## The Duomo and Leaning Tower of Pisa

Pisa is situated farther down the Arno River from Florence and about six miles inland from the Mediterranean Sea. Pisa is famous as the birthplace of Galileo and especially for its splendid trio of architectural masterpieces, the Duomo, the Baptistery, and of course, the world-famous Leaning Tower. They all stand near each other on the same site called the "Field of Miracles." They all have galleries of narrow columns decorated with marble inlay work, showing the influence of the Islamic world and of the Eastern Christian world. Pisa traded with both these regions.

The Duomo was built first. Finally, the famous tower was begun in 1173. It stands 190 feet tall and is made of white marble. Bonnano Pisano, the engineer in charge, had completed three of its eight stories when the uneven settling of the building's foundation on the soft ground became noticeable. Scientists and engineers have tried to find solutions for many years. In 1990 the tower was in grave danger of collapsing and closed to the public. The Leaning Tower still stands, but no one knows for how long. Perhaps you will be the engineer who will find the perfect solution for its preservation.

# Important Dates

**From the Foundation of the city to the Carolingian Age** • Florence began as a colony established by Julius Caesar for veterans of the Roman army in 59 B.C. At first, Florence, or Florentia, meaning "the flourishing town," was not a large and important place. However, it soon had temples and theaters, baths and an aqueduct. By the third century A.D., Florence had become the provincial capital of the Roman Empire and an important crossroads and trade center. During the fifth and sixth centuries, Florence was invaded by hoards of barbarians. As a result, the city suffered a period of decline. Only with the arrival of the Franks in the ninth century did Florence begin to develop again.

**After the Year One Thousand** • During the period of the struggles between the Roman Empire and the Papacy (1076–1122), the city became increasingly more independent from imperial power but found itself at the center of bitter struggles with neighboring cities and with landowners linked to the emperor. For this reason, Florence sided with the Pope who had trusted the Florentine bankers and merchants with the collection of taxes and tributes in Italy and in regions on the other side of the Alps. In 1125, Florence attacked Fiesole and conquered the ancient city after a long seige.

**The Period of The Florentine Commune** • During the twelfth century, noble families had a strong influence on the governing institutions in Florence. The city ruled itself and gradually became a city-state. Its economic power continued to grow and its prestige spread across Europe thanks to the florin, a gold coin minted in the city, and to the skill of its bankers and merchants.

In 1215, during a marriage dispute, a young nobleman was stabbed to death on the Ponte Vecchio. Groups of Florentines became increasingly hostile toward each other. Family hatred grew into political hatred. The two parties were known as the Guelphs, friends of the Church, and the Ghibellines, friends of the Empire. Political struggles dominated the whole inner life of the city from the second half of the thirteenth century to the beginning of the fourteenth century. Yet throughout this period the city continued to grow in size, population, and territory, and its economy and cultural importance continued to increase. In 1246, Santa Maria Novella, the first of the great Florentine churches, was begun. Between 1331 and 1338, Florence conquered Pistoia and Arezzo, and in 1406 Florence overcame Pisa which gave it an extremely important outlet to the sea that it needed for its commerce.

**The Medici Family** • In 1434 Cosimo de' Medici became Lord of Florence, but he did not undertake any official administrative position. At his death in 1464, he was succeeded by his son Piero both as businessman and as political leader of Florence. However, it was under Piero's son, Lorenzo, that the city experienced its most successful period. In that time of relative peace, the city's cultural and artistic life flowered too, thanks to Lorenzo de' Medici's generous patronage of the arts. When Lorenzo died in 1492, he had made Florence the most powerful city in Italy. The Medici family virtually ruled Florence for about a century, but never officially took any public office or title.

**The Grand-Duchy of Tuscany** • Florence experienced a brief period as a republic, then, in 1530, the Medici returned to Florence and in 1569, Cosimo I became Grand Duke of Tuscany. He boosted the economy by promoting the construction of a fleet and beginning the drainage of the malaria-infested marshes in the Maremma region. His successors continued his work until 1737, when, with the death of Giovanni Gastone de'Medici, the Medici dynasty came to an end.

**The Dukes of Lorraine** • The Grand Duchy of Florence passed into the House of Lorraine, first with Francis (1737–1765), the son of Leopold of Hapsburg, the Duke of Lorraine and later with Duke Peter Leopold (1765-1792). Peter Leopold encouraged several reforms both in the areas of state administration and in the justice system. He promoted the drainage of the Chiana Valley, founded academies, universities, and museums and was the first sovereign in Europe to abolish the death penalty.

# Glossary

**alum** a white mineral used in the processes of dying cloth or tanning animal hides and skins

**arte** or corporazione, a guild or trade association

**barile** a unit of measure for wine

**Berlingaccio** the last Thursday of the annual Carnival, a public holiday in Florence

**Calimala** the oldest guild in Florence, the Cloth Merchants' Guild, whose patron saint was St. John the Baptist

**capital** the top part of a column, often decorated in different ways

**chiasse** or chiassette an extremely narrow alley

**comestio** the first meal of the day, eaten before 11 A.M.

**Commune** a council that weights serious matters of state

**corporazione** see arte above

**discepoli** laborers in a craftsman's workshop who have completed their apprenticeship and have become assistants to a master craftsman

**fresco** a painting or design made by painting with watercolors on wet plaster

**gabelliere** a civil servant who collects the taxes on goods at the city gates

**loggia** an arched gallery built into or projecting from the side of a building

**lucco** a hooded garment made of woolen cloth, reaching down to the feet, and worn without a belt. It is worn mainly by older people, magistrates, doctors, and jurists

**mazzocchio** a head covering made of a length of twisted woolen cloth, wound around the head in a loose ring, worn at an angle, with one end free to fall over a shoulder

**mezzetta** the smallest unit of liquid measure

**navata** the aisles inside a church, separated by columns or pillars

**navicello** a flat-bottomed boat, used for transporting goods on the Arno River

**palazzo** a palace

**patron** a person, usually wealthy and influencial, who sponsors and supports an individual, activity, or institution associated with the arts or sciences

**piazza** in Italy, an open public square, especially one surrounded by buildings

**prandium** evening dinner, the most important meal of the day in Florence, eaten before the sun sets

**Signoria** the governing body of Florence in the 15th century

**spezerie** apothecary shops, or pharmacies, in 15th century Florence

**sporti** a kind of closed covered balcony, made from wood or brick, jutting out from the facade of a house

**staioro a corda** a measure of area

**tabernacola** a shrine erected as an expression of religious devotion

**tiratoio** a place near the dyer's workshop, where the pieces of dyed cloth are hung out to dry and acquire the required shape

**torsell** a twisted length of woolen cloth

# Further Reading

Foster, Leila M. *Italy*. (Overview series). Lucent Books, 1998.

Green, Jen. *Michaelangelo*. (Famous Artists series). Barron, 1994.

Hausam, Josephine S. *Italy*. (Countries of the World). Gareth Stevens, Inc., 1999.

Hightower, Paul W. *Galileo: Astronomer and Physicist*. (Great Minds of Science series). Enslow Publications, 1997.

Marshall, Norman F., and Ripamonti, Aldo. *Leonardo da Vinci*. (What Made Them Great series). Silver Burdett Press, 1990.

Mason, Antony, and Hughs, Andrew S. *Leonardo da Vinci*. (Famous Artists series). Barron, 1998.

Perdrizet, Marie-Pierre. *The Cathedral Builders*. (Peoples of the Past series). Millbrook Press, 1992.

Petit, Jayne. *Michelangelo: Genius of the Renaissance*. (Impact Biography series). Watts, 1998.

Powell, Katherine. *Italy*. (Origins series). Watts, 1998.

Reeves, Marjorie. *Florence in the Time of the Medici*. (Then and There series). Longman, 1982.

White, Michael. *Galileo Galilei: Inventor, Astronomer, and Rebel*. (Giants of Science series). Blackbirch, 1999.

# Index